THE
SKYLARK
SINGS

Random Notes on
Loss, Lies and Love

WILLIS McCREE

GLASS**SPIDER**PUBLISHING

Edited by Jonathan Clark
Cover design by Judith S. Design & Creativity
www.judithsdesign.com
Published by Glass Spider Publishing
www.glassspiderpublishing.com

Sometimes we float along with conceptual definitions of what love is without forming concrete images of love. Living in a fantasy world of what love should be, how it should be expressed and what our lovers should be and do can undermine finding real love.

The quest for love in my life has left me wondering if I'll ever really know what love is. I've had amazing connections, been lied to, and lost the feeling of loving someone. I will never give up on the hope that my love will be reciprocated with the same intensity I give it. To those who have loved me, I am grateful and better for that love even when it did not last.

"The greatest thing you'll ever learn is just to love and be loved in return."–Eden Ahbez

For D.S.

CONTENTS

INTRODUCTION

YOU KNOW ME.. 15

SECTION I: MURMURATIONS

FINDING THE NANDINA 19

FALL 20

LYING WITH NATURE 21

MARKS OF LIFE 22

REVELATIONS 23

ARTIST LOVER 25

WIDOW'S WEB 26

AS I LEAVE 27

TORN 28

IS IT ENOUGH 29

TRUE FREEDOM 30

AWAITING FIRE 32

LIVING ON 33

SECTION II: EXALTATIONS

SKYLARK 37

TWO SPOONS 38

LET US PRAY.. 40

NO LIMITS 41

UNDER THE TABLE... 42

THE AFTERNOON 43

MORNING SHOWERS... 44

IS THERE A TIME 46

I WILL.. 47

REMEMBER ME 48

I THOUGHT.. 49

LOVE CANNOT BE DEFINED 51

SECTION III: FLEDGLINGS

A GLANCE... 57

UNSPOKEN WORDS.. 59

WALK AT FERNWOOD 60

CHASING THE MOON... 62

WORLDS APART.. 63

WEDNESDAY 65

PARACHUTE.. 66

BLACK DOG 67

BABY.. 68

KISS ME IN THE RAIN 69

IT COMES 70

I WILL WONDER 71

MURMURATION OF WISHES 72

MEMORIES MAY SCATTER 73

SECTION IV: CHATTERINGS

MY OPEN HEART... 77

GRACE GROWS 78

SPEEDING AWAY 80

TIN ROOF RHYTHM.. 82

SCHOOL BOY 83

THROUGH THE WINDOW 84

NEBULA 85

THAT FEELING.. 86

SEA OF HONEST LOVE... 88

PLANTINGS.. 90

SEEDS... 91

LAST LOVE 92

SECOND CHANCE 94

MY AGE 96

CONCLUSION

THE KNOCK.. 101

INTRODUCTION

YOU KNOW ME

An angry lover once told me I
would not be loved once
the real me was known.
That I
would not have anyone long.

Love, been chasing it
all my life.
I have felt it,
found it, lost it,
and it
has forged along
leaving me in a
wake of pleasure when we skinny dipped in the
lake.
Unmet expectations, wanting kisses that never
happened.
Romantic gestures like
watching *Breakfast at Tiffany's* on Christmas
morning,
hope that was unanswered like my phone calls.

I will not give up
hope or expectations,
without them
my head hangs a little lower,
my heart fills with empty sighs.
Love,
you know me.

SECTION I

MURMURATIONS
Revelations and Ruminations

FINDING THE NANDINA

Planted a nandina on the sheltered
side of the house,
found it driving on country backroads.

In the sunlight elsewhere
Maw Maw's pot stood filled with portulaca.

Abandoned houses, gravel roads, shovels,
gardens becoming fallow fields,
untended yards,
flowers, shrubs, trees we looted,
relocated them to a garden menagerie of our own.

A bearded man appeared on a porch,
the house caving in.
A deep, scary, raspy voice–
he said, *leave my frogs alone*.

Pillaged an old barber chair once
near Aunt Bessie's house,
hauled it home
up the stairs to my room,
spilled oil from the hydraulic reservoir,
pumped it up and sat in it for years.

While outside, grew the nandina my mother
loved.

FALL

Sky the color
of cornflowers in the garden,
their movement the movement
of the few clouds above,

both moved by currents
of crisp, honey-scented air
that tussles my hair
lying under the apple tree in the backyard.

Silently counting red delicious,
I wonder things
I'll never know
about gravity, the universe.

Just happy I could
think of the questions
and that
fall is upon me.

LYING WITH NATURE

Naked flesh against hard stone
sunlight cascades like the waterfall nearby,
a red-tailed hawk circles in lapis sky

with marbled eyes and fluid feather
caught on the wind's tongue–
looks down on me.

Breezes blow over me
I lie there, smile,
realize we are lost
in wild beauty.

We explode together
amid nature's brilliant delight.

MARKS OF LIFE

In our house
ashtrays
filled with ash,
cigarette butts,
like gravestones

in the church yard.
Markers of lives,
statements of how they began,
were lived,
how they ended.

Cigarette butts, too,
statements of lives ending.

An armadillo caught,
put in a cage.
What were we thinking
taking it back to Kentucky?

It died trying to escape
being our pet,
as we sat and ate.
The cage and corpse
in the garbage behind the café.
We drove away from its
life,
marked by a trash can.

REVELATIONS

They can be dangerous,
revelations
about ourselves, our
lovers, our world.

As if waking from the solid sleep of
a midday nap, realize we
have been possessed,
our bodies, souls,
hearts belong to another.

Helplessness, that's what revelations
paint, splatters of color in the hair, the floor.
They show us there is no
controlling others, what they make of life.

Our hearts beat for someone else,
keep time with another heart,
like the pendulum of the clock on my office wall,
and they tear as easily as tissue when
we are betrayed and
pump loudly when we come together.

Joined, pathways in life hiked
up a mountain or along farmland,
finally crossed, and a fusion
of souls
makes us one with another.

Careful of loitering inside
your mind, revelations float past
like newspapers blowing in the wind
and seeds of thought are planted
to sprout like unwanted grass in a flower bed
when we know to bury
the great contradictions we live.

Revelations shine down brightly,
like a buttery golden, orange moon
beckoning us forward
to our destinies, swept
upward to become who we
have always been.

ARTIST LOVER

Every painted stroke
brushes against my face as
the artist creates a painting
modeled by love for me.

Water colored handiwork
captures the texture of my lips,
shows the subtle way
to wash away the outside world.

Applied acrylic,
sinews shown,
crimson stain on paper
becomes an abstract lover's sketch.

We lie upon blankets
two souls on canvas
keeping warm,
the fresco of our lives unfolding.

Through bold, blended strokes–
deep, dark painted
recessed eyelet pools
reflect sweet gaze.

I inhale the artist
whose soul blends with mine,
framed in the arms of an
impassioned embrace.

WIDOW'S WEB

Love erupted three times last night
in pleasured, brilliant flames
each time I whispered my
lover's name.

Among sheets of saffron chenille
we lay as one entwined
resplendent, naked form
held in the web your heart spun.

Red hour glass in hand
kisses, sticky wet
nectar, poison to my tongue
paralyzed in love's embrace.

Wrapped in your arms,
a spider's web of tangled limbs.
And as the spider eats its mate,
I too become

a hollow shell.
Afterwards, wanting to be more,
I find I am only
prey you have trapped.

AS I LEAVE

The plane rises from the steamy tarmac,
leaps through cotton candied skies
dirtied by smog and rain.
The pilot left me standing in darkness.

I carry just one bag
coat in hand, the only memento
the taste of his lips.
His eyes, hair
inky black, pulled me into
a darkness I never wanted to leave.

But as light pushes away
the night and the next day begins,
I stand to board my own plane,
return to life
without those dark eyes
pulling me in, holding me
as he held me yesterday,
the day before, made love to me
then told me I wasn't rich
enough for him.
I leave,
fly, homeward.

TORN

I tried to love others, but
you were the only woman
my mind and body
connected to, worked with.
One firefly lit night,
Said, *I love you pumpkin*
a quick witted reply
Love you squash, and
the deal and our lives
were sealed on the back steps
of your father's house.

Miles later, anger and
heated words, you
storm out the back door
with me in hot pursuit.
My shirt catches on the door,
tearing the sleeve of
our matching football jerseys.

We stare at the rip, burst into
simultaneous laughter,
roll in the grass breathless,
as anger disappears through a torn space.

IS IT ENOUGH

What is left when I allow my own
shallow pretense to be burned away,
as I contemplate my life, my ability to love and
rise above my own needs?
I sit alone in the dark morning and counsel myself
on this,
drone philosophical as I tend to do
every early morning as I depart the night.

Will it be enough to sustain a future?
Can I shed the weight? Selfish feelings
become something strong, we are
stronger with trust and forgiveness.

Is it enough to love, or must one be in love
for sweet, night pillow talk
days together
the choice of friends
how we behave?

I leave it to my heart
to answer.

TRUE FREEDOM

My wife said freedom requires complete
accountability
from me, her, all of us.
There is pain in the
muck of a divorce.

I struggle to take my own medicine,
see what I have seen,
what I have inflicted, what has been inflicted on
me,
decide what I love more,
the everything, the lovely, or the mean.

Not sure of her choice,
but I choose the everything,
I choose not to dwell on
the mean.

Will she carry the burden of
the ghosts she thrust upon me,
work to remove them from us both?
She called so many friends, co-workers
trying to find infidelity when
there was none.

This is not how we die,
not in anger, mistrust, betrayal–
not in the throes of all this.
Let us be free, move past this.
Let us end this together,
walk out of this fog to
freedom.

AWAITING FIRE

Repentance–
please fall on me,
search the ashes,
dig into the pit,
turn them over in my hand.

No hint of
future fire
upon a stone hearth,
hoping embers burst
into life.
Impassioned flames,
they've withered away
into a grave.

I've waited by
another's fire,
warm,
hoping life
has not left me
cold, shrunken, alone.

LIVING ON

Dark house,
like my cup of coffee.
Whisps
of heat,

like a marsh I
saw once
driving in the early fall.
The air

cooler than the swamp,
water slowly giving up
its warm soul,
turning into a cold corpse.

I sip warmth, find I
too am slowly giving up
my warmth. Yet I
live on and somewhere

I will find I have outlived
my losses, my lies, my loves.

SECTION II

EXALTATIONS
Spirals and Sparks

SKYLARK

The sun wakes,
day turns pink,
blue,
and you are all my thoughts.

My mind wonders
where you are.
My heart, it
does not wonder.

If I live a day,
a million years,
I cannot love you
more than this moment.

But for fluttering
wings, hearts,
time stands still,
as beneath my feet
the skylark launches,
spirals and sings.

TWO SPOONS

Noise of 24th Street
softly floats in
on cool, morning air
chilled like good wine.

Zebra like shadows cast
gray stripes, as
we snuggle deep
beneath down-filled comfort.

Sounds bounce off red sponge-painted walls
softened by yellow light,
as early sun peaks
at us over skyscrapers.

Horns blast, motors race,
the street stretches to life, yet
we hold on to our night
perched above it all.

We stir, lie back down,
Liquid-mercury,
the warm spots of our bodies
refill the mattress.

The absence of cat's purrs
fills our minds,
lost him yesterday after
twenty years of petting, jealous meows.

And through the blinds,
two spoons,
perfectly tucked together,
hold the city at bay.

LET US PRAY

You left me holding a searing hot pan
of images, burning
my heart, eyes.

Selfish acts, no thought of me,
no thought of repercussions,
leaving me at that bar
to find my own way home.

Jealousy made you someone else,
made us something we are not.
I walked home in the rain,
a drenched duck, waddling
in streets of anger.

Kneel with me, speak a
prayer of redemption,
self-forgiveness, my forgiveness,
God's forgiveness.

Let us pray
that we can save us
in this world of
concrete boxes and
never ending traffic.

NO LIMITS

Alone, together–
gloves, that's what we are.
Hearts, hands,
bodies, and souls

fitting as no other.
We make a pizza,
chopping, pouring wine,
not talking, just together.

No limits in love,
no reason to cut the bake short.
Out of the oven, the smell, basil,
a remembrance of a time
in Saint Mark's Square, pigeons.

I give you the first bite,
lips parted, we kiss
marinara, we are
just an extension of
one another.

UNDER THE TABLE

You just home,
we stop on the kitchen steps,
clothes shed like fall leaves
littering beneath the tree.
You called me Tree.

Our lips touch
our hearts race, blood pumps.
We spiral
to the kitchen floor.
Cool linoleum.

We lay entwined,
two giggling people,
my arm
through the rung of the chair,
looking up at the bottom of the kitchen table.

THE AFTERNOON

How different the afternoon
had you but kissed me.
I leaned down–my lips warm.

Just silence
from you, my anger, lunch alone,
naps apart, nothing shared:
thoughts, needs.

No laughter, the
only thing to do is
avoid each other,
keep the pathways clear.

You didn't apologize for
your rejection
just sat in front of the television.

Your words leaving me
an amputee
with heart cut out, holding it
in a hand that doesn't exist.

MORNING SHOWERS

Little drops of blue doubt
creep into my head,
rain drops hitting the patio,
one dark spot at a time
until the whole thing is wet.

I step out into the morning
naked like me,
the shower
warm, refreshing.
A wild turkey in the backyard
squats over her chicks as
rain continues.

Doubts, like
the thunder overhead, are
the price I pay
for this peaceful life.

Built a stone wall, planted gourds,
hung a hammock
you wouldn't use.
I push on knowing the only certain thing,
uncertainty.

The sky clears, the shower done
I sit bare,
watching crystal blue
step away from clouds,
frosty sea glass,
smooth, tumbled,
striped beach towels
hovering overhead.

Someday a chipmunk will
hide corn kernels in the cracks
of that wall,
they'll sprout and without doubt
push on.

IS THERE A TIME

Sitting in the desert heat, I think maybe it never
has been.
Once maybe, when
you held my hand as we walked into Escena Grill,
or when you dropped your clothes and
without hesitation jumped in the pool with me.

You say you have nothing to give,
but you took me to Paris, gave up smoking
let me be a Canary in the mornings
while you had your coffee,
held me when my son died.

Don't like lots of touching, but enough,
you have my back, eat my cooking
let me have him.
You stay with me through
my eccentric days, help calm my mind.

Simple things, no grand gestures,
they are what I do.
Valentine's chocolates, yellow roses from the
market,
endless energy to make you happy
and unless you are, I do not know love.

I WILL

fight for the one I love,
slice a sword sharp-ravenous,
slid from its sheath
into those who would come between us,
powerful, murderous,
a quick death or
sliced away slowly,
their entrails pouring out over hands
that tried to hurt,
their eyes watching the last drop of blood pool,
push them to the ground,
raise a shield to
keep you safe, protected
from those who would
take advantage of a heart
revealing itself as does a bright, cloudless day,
throw a lasso of love
around you and keep it taut,
so you are not dragged away,
punch a gut, face, or groin,
render agony and pain
to give you time to run
safely back into my arms
wrapped around you each night,
keep the nightmares of the past at bay
spend the rest of my life
giving you my heart, my love, my life.

REMEMBER ME

We saw the hummingbird dance
nearly twenty years ago.
It seems my mind lives
a singular life, since
the moment I fell in love with you,
no time has since passed

to us,
to the love I feel.
Like birds, we
soared high when young
drop closer to the earth
with each year that loops.

My arms,
a nest of love,
holds you,
waiting, knowing our souls are
spun inside, growing wings
to fill the world with color,
a kaleidoscopic flight.

Remember who you fell in love with,
tell me, touch me, let the scent of rain
fill the world with song that
remembers me.

I THOUGHT

For a year your family's hatred
wore me away like driftwood
on a lonely beach.

Our agreement: I would pretend to
be involved in an extramarital
relationship, pretend you were
an innocent bystander.

You, afraid of the judgments
they so loudly pronounce, let them slash at me.
I thought you loved me
enough to have my back.

You shuddered, tried to avoid
threw me under the bus
your sister drove,
yelling, accusing,
both of you drunk at dinner,
painting me unfaithful.

You let her scream at me in my own house,
shrugged, but next morning
you stood, shaking in front of the kitchen sink
as the man I knew, and
told the truth on the subject,

and we are good together,
happy.
You are the man
I thought you were.

LOVE CANNOT BE DEFINED

A crack in broken tile.
I stub my toe,
curse.
One long hair in an eyebrow cascading
over me,
blocking my sight from anything else,
only seeing it, you,
all else in the background–
your name, your voice,
my voice calling out on frosty mornings,
dark,
quiet, waiting for the sun,
streaking light through the blinds,
waterfall of a dawn,
hearing you snore,
dirty socks on the floor,
smelly.
Scent of how we were yesterday,
questions, anger, no answers,
trying to get out of the corner
I've painted myself into,
wanting
you to paint,
paint a picture of us together.
Laughter, pillow talk,
shiny hair leaving residue on
crisp cotton,

seeing the spot tomorrow,
knowing your arms, my hands,
lips,
eyes sparkle with wonder,
photos taken with a new camera
stacked black and white against the wall,
your shoes stacked too,
slippers with the backs crushed down,
no leash to hold these dogs in,
freedom–
every man needs it.
Do what you have to do,
I do too, knowing my love is true.
Not a traitor,
holding the line,
a skyscraper of thoughts,
fears,
feeble attempts at being
more than humanly possible,
putting you first in line,
the biggest piece of pie on your plate,
last drop of soymilk,
lifting more than my share,
giving,
wanting, gnawing desires
further than mind and flesh,
ungodly controlling the universe,

a black hole, really,
no cosmos can contain the want,
need,
happiness only at yours.
A stone wall surrounding
protecting.
Helping you put on your socks
when your knee hurts too badly to lift,
lifting us into a universe that's
imploding or exploding or whatever it does
around this blue dot we share.
Air kisses
when distance separates our lips,
trusting there is light beyond darkness,
nestling when we return.
Count backwards from any place,
stop at one, because
you are the one,
the hand in my glove,
walking quietly, birdsong adrift.
A gravel road,
super highway, a long-traveled fare,
and the simple,
steady
beating of my heart.

SECTION III

FLEDGLINGS
Magpies and Goodbyes

A GLANCE

You left me on the sidewalk
that November day I glanced your way,
whispered your name. Our
first meeting, not sure what
would happen.
Fell on cold, hard stone

head spinning, splitting,
pavement splashed red
with all my thoughts and fears
my heart bursting.

The lusts, desires and longings
scampered at your feet.
Upraised arms, waiting
to be held,
feel the heartbeat that gave them life.

The earth stopped
frozen on its axis–like me,
breathless vacuum
no time, space, light.

Celestial bodies
burned brighter,
ashamed they'd not shone
upon your face.

Eyes green, gold flecks,
molten light
burning through
me.

If the sun falls, the moon burns,
all I've known
vanishes.

I glance back,
my shattered shell
lies on the sidewalk
where I first whispered your name.

UNSPOKEN WORDS

Clear summer light,
raw ivory silk, your skin
spun into perfection,
like a perfect peach
two spheres
sharing a heart,
a single core.

Spanish hazel,
Scottish grey
eyes boring into the recesses of us,
hovering gently, pure, exquisite tenderness.

No need for whispered words, nor those
formed within our minds,
known but not spoken.
We, the only ones skilled
to decipher.

Our love a flickering candle,
still, noble, tender.
We know the sweetness of two souls
merging, never properly returning
to singular existence.

Hold me, don't speak, move,
embrace me, stay with me,
take one step and
leap into the vast unknown.

WALK AT FERNWOOD

Footprints in snow, crunching, leaving them
behind us,
holding hands, walking in a frozen tree tunnel
running, I try to catch your breath in cold air.

You laugh at the impossible effort,
tuft of dead grass escaping the snow hoping for
spring, life,
like us, hoping for love to bloom as the earth
greens.

The gray wool coat I bought you matching the
winter sky
draped over us, we stand above the valley
lost in the inversion, trusting
there are lights shining somewhere in that thick
haze.

Trusting there is love somewhere as we sort out
unknown
spaces between us, this
quiet moment of togetherness, tender, motionless
only Magpies and our hearts making noise.

Stood there one spring night when you were
away,
spoke your name in air so crisp it
sliced the words.

Crawling insects, oaks budding green, growing,
awaiting renewal, and we walk Fernwood
remembering
all hope bursting forth, leafing into the hope love
defines.

CHASING THE MOON

Pre-dawn blue
clouds separate
the moon drops.
A beacon lowered,
like you dropping beneath my covers–
moon, sun, stars all in one.

I wait until you come home,
lay beneath my daylight,
surrender your heart and soul,
you already have mine.

The day rushes
quickly, dawn then dusk,
my empty bed,
cold, lonely
until you return,
a moonbeam in the dark.

I ravish you
like prey,
a wild beast starving
under a full moon.

Devoured.

WORLDS APART

Rain falls outside the window
wind, soft gusts
through the pines. They
whisper of you, and you are unaware
in your locked away world.

Crickets chirp,
grass grows,
birds begin to stir.
Dawn is upon me, but you have
monitored light 24 hours a day.

All of us unaware the world spins,
hoot, hoot, hoot, the owl
in the tree outside and I
speak our loneliness.

My heart beats, waits,
the worlds we live in continue.
You have not read the words
I penned while you were away,
and most likely never will, or

one day when I'm dead
and you are feeling guilty,
you may read and wish,
but then it will be too late.

And you'll say to yourself, as
you did to me every time you
hurt me, *Let the past be in the past,*
and then you will know how
impossible that is.

WEDNESDAY

It's Wednesday, not the weekend,
not May 31st when you are released, just
Wednesday.
The day I spend making a list,
choosing exactly what Wednesday wears.
Focusing only on visiting you
behind bullet proof glass at the jail.

I need to live in this day,
wasted so many Wednesday's
waiting for you to come home,
reliving the officers standing beside you,
handcuffs on your wrists,
counting the minutes, hours,
till another Wednesday wakes.

Another Wednesday, anxiety, longing,
love that did not waste away
or leave me to deal with life alone.

When will Wednesday find you
in my arms, making love all Wednesday
not wasting the day.

It's Wednesday, this is the day I live.

PARACHUTE

In the distant parking lot, I sit in my car
not supposed to be there,
waiting for a glimpse of you.
The night not yet chased away
watching as the white police van
comes to life.

Slowly, those going to community service
file out of the jail,
penguins walking with their shackles clanking.

You said once through thick glass
how dehumanizing it is each day
to return, be forced to strip naked
as a newly hatched bird and bend, cough,

jump and shake before the jailer,
bare bulbed lights shining
down on your transgressions.
Total submission to an ineffective
check for smuggled contraband.

I told you once at visitation,
When you falter, look up to
the cornflower expanse above, and
think of my love as a blue parachute sky
that floats you safely back to me.

BLACK DOG

I saw a black dog
sitting at the road,
wagged his tail like we were friends,
bit me when I tried to feed him,
make him my own.

Thought about kicking the black dog
for the pain he made, knew
many others had abused him, hurt him.
Decided instead to stand by him,
bathe him, take him home.

He came too, curled up by my fire,
let me feed him, love him.
I put the collar on the porch,
gave him freedom.

He stayed, recovered,
became a playful pup, but
always sat looking down the road.

I told him I knew.

One day I pointed,
he wagged his tail
and started down the road.

BABY

Nicknamed him Baby
after the Driver, walked
at Fernwood, took him into our arms
our hearts, our home.

We said weed was okay,
he listened, used it, then
the age-old question; if
someone jumped would he,
and he jumped off the bridge
to a harder place, harder drugs
that took him away.

There is a line
we can't get past,
can't give up support
can't just turn away
say we don't care,
then tell him we'll see.

Took him in
groomed, dressed him,
gave ourselves.
When he didn't bend,
we almost walked away
but didn't.

KISS ME IN THE RAIN

You heard it first–
rain dancing on the roof,
my ears catching up,
my heart racing.

Up from dinner, you
reached, took my hand,
I said, *what*, you said, *nothing*.

Out the door, down the steps,
the patio below
a wet dance floor,

the dance began,
embracing,
dancing alongside
all those raindrops.

Your head on my shoulder,
you whispered,
Sing our song to me.
I began, *Come on, kiss me in the rain.*
And you did.

IT COMES

It comes
in the night breeze,
a silent goodbye.
You are leaving, mind
and heart already gone,
the rest of you will follow.

It comes
in empty spaces,
on your pillow
now,
dead, dark, empty.

It comes
in the ache
you no longer feel or fill.
Your affection for me
evaporated like virga
in the desert distance.

It comes
in broken promises,
me, someone else
both believing,
you are theirs alone.

I WILL WONDER

Is love an entitlement
giving us rights, freedoms
with others, within ourselves?

Or a responsibility
to hold our lovers closer, guard
them as a treasure not wasted.
Sprouting in tender gardens,
given warm milk, like a
stray kitten, loved, cherished, protected.

A look in the mirror after
betrayal, honestly assessing
the deceit.
Do eyes look into themselves,
or skim over and cloud memory?

Are those memories
happy ones? When held, do
we wish to be elsewhere?

Can I hear words, sweet or sour
and not want to slap you quiet?
Does love require forgiveness,
anger, an answer?

MURMURATION OF WISHES

If wishes were sunshine,
skies would always be blue
like the Indigo Buntings at
the feeder. We'd
never have rain.
I'd wake to the bright light of love.

If wishes were birds,
great flocks in murmuration
on the wing would
fly wild, free, and strong.

If wishes were words,
five syllables, more,
or a single flight,
I'd whisper your name
till love was the only word.

MEMORIES MAY SCATTER

But I will not forget your smile,
the golden flecks in your hazel eyes, that glance,
the silky curls of your dark hair, the wrinkles by
your ears when you laugh,
the softness of your whispers at night, my breath
on your neck,
the tenderness of your shoulder when I bite,
the taste of your lips, the bite on my lower lip,
the smell of you,
the uncontrollable growls, the lassos of love,
the blanket on the grass,
the Sandhill Cranes in Nebraska,
the feel of my ginger arms around you, pressed
against you
whispering, *Baby,* the way I bent to kiss you the
first time,
laying between your bowed legs, monkey toes
pinching me,
Fernwood at night or snowy daylight,
November 22, or to tell you every day I love you,
how it feels to love you as I do,
to die in your arms.

SECTION IV

CHATTERINGS
Gulls and Choughs

MY OPEN HEART

An empty satchel but
for bits of torn life,
scraps of lovers, pieces of their lives,
our attempts at life away from
the outside world,
opened by my wandering mind.

A book
ready to be read by
hungry eyes
or browsed in disinterest,
to be held for a moment,
anticipating a full read
or a few pages ruffled.

A rare, golden bird
caged by few, door left open
but flightless,
it cannot escape.

Laundry, hanging like window curtains
fluttering, like gulls in the breeze.
So many things words
cannot express,
only feelings within the thrumming
as I stand,
on the edge of my life.

GRACE GROWS

On the balcony of your apartment
scarlet bougainvillea, potted,
warmed by afternoon sun
gift of sweet *tete-a-tete*.

We named her Grace one night
when candlelight stars twinkled,
the bottoms of our bare feet touching,
reclined on rattan.

Grace's ancestors grow up garden walls,
shading us as we sit on a veranda in *Distrito
Federal*
one lazy afternoon, where
we talk of missing our siesta.

You sip *aqua fresca* but it's iced tea for your
gringo.
I wore the yellow shirt you didn't like
to the restaurant
where you ordered for me,
made fun of the young, blonde man.

Later, tucked inside each other's arms,
bananas foster on our lips,
memories of Mexico and your grandfather's
hacienda,
we fall open like a robe

tied loosely at the waist, not concealing
the differences that unravel us.
A scarlet reminder hangs over the balcony,
Grace
waves to me as I go.

SPEEDING AWAY

He says I look so sexy
and gently touches my arm.
No harm, I guess in talking to a stranger
who says I'm what he's looking for.

Too enraptured to see him as he is
we walk to his car, he's drunk, I'm intoxicated,
drive his Porsche into the night,
thinking this might be my chance at love.

I look above streetlights
to his penthouse and think I am home.
As we sweat the night away
the lights of Century City blaze hot
like us, embraced by ocean and Pacific Palisades
nestled in public greenery of the night.

Brown skin so sweet, I taste mocha,
I rise and fall, dig deep into him,
rise to breathe,
let him breathe.

Screams.

At will I take him over the edge,
like driving down the 405,
alive with pleasure, traffic
stops, then races westward to the sea,
while along his body's coast we drive
at break neck speed,
never worrying about corners, cliffs or mountains.

I step out, fall off,
discarded, a spoiled rich kid
reaching past safety of self-imposed walls,
using another kind of Daddy.

TIN ROOF RHYTHM

In the cabin loft, we hear
rain, splatters on tin roof above,
we lie under blankets, printed with moose
images.

Rain, it is my love song,
speaks to me, envelops me,
takes me far beyond physical longing.
It can be slow, steady, matching our bodies
together
or become a down pour,
a clap of thunder, torrential passion too.

A rhythm on the tin drum above,
the night closes around us,
we match its closeness
and fall into it
and each other.

SCHOOL BOY

We met by happenstance
or universal alignment,
shifting sands.

Said, *Hello*,
you flashed a smile–
innocence, want.

Became a school boy,
tongue tied,
finches in flight just
like in the 6th grade when I first
felt love.

Time marches on,
a swift enemy,
love makes me feel young again,
and I'm still a school boy

wanting you for my own.

THROUGH THE WINDOW

I stand outside and peer
through the window,
we are celebrating our commitment
with friends, family,
but alcohol and cocaine have taken
you between the thighs of
another man,

life pumping between you.
What is lacking in life
that you are never filled,
always hungry, that you would
forget the words just spoken,
the promises made?

Watching you sends ocean waves, quaking of the
earth,
my brain exploding,
shotgun blasts shooting
me full of holes
that cannot be filled, empty
like your tuxedo lying on the floor.

You are there, alive
with him, while I
stand dead outside
and wonder why.

NEBULA

Dusted the sills of
your fingerprints this morning
left by the death of our star,
exploding gases and clouds.
A spot where you put your head,
greasy window mark.

Looking out the window now,
wrenching stomach for
what you did last night
to me,
to us.

I pick up bedding,
your tux limp, like the commitments
you spoke, broken arrows on the ground
never flying forward.

I'll return it, while the washer
churns off the stains and smells
that crush me.

THAT FEELING

when you see a wave racing toward you,
know you can't get out of its way,
that it's going to wash over you, turn your
world dark and confusing.

How helpless you are when
an egg is rolling off the counter,
you're not quick enough to catch it
before it shatters, splattering everywhere.

The acidic taste
just before things start spinning and
violent streams of vomit explode,
nothing can plug it,
soften the volcanic flow.

How worthless you feel when
your love takes drunken liberties,
pretense of loving you pulled into the air,
getting up, leaving as soon as it's over,
stepping out the door, alone, bruised.

Life created, controlled,
a lover who doesn't want to be my lover,
sends no roses, nor pushes himself
to be a truer man.

Sulking darkened skies
behind a frowning, uninterested face,
sits behind curtains blocking light,
no effort after his betrayals,
my heartaches.

I wait for the egg to shatter
vomit to form, the wave
to wash me away.
A preparation of sorts, knowing,
I barricade my heart, shore up my emotions,
remember I have given a good fight,
all humanly possible,
my everything. Knowing
not all love is meant to last.

SEA OF HONEST LOVE

In a sea of almost loved,
is it better
to float along or drown,
pulled down
by those
who I wanted to love me?

Regrets
washing up on tomorrow's shore,
drift wood of life
that might have been
if I hadn't
held back.

Like gulls crying above the water,
we said things we needed to hear,
heard those things we wanted
said. Empty shells
buried
here in the sand.

They lie, waiting for
waves to take them away
to depths where
they cannot be recovered,

nor can we.
The sea claims us,
keeps us
from the light of
honest love.

PLANTINGS

Grain fields, heads bowed,
move with wind,
they have no control,
nor I. We plant
far gone fields in hopes
of sustenance.

My true love
strayed, leaving
me a cityscape
of sorrow. He left me
to explore
high rises of others.

Shall I walk concrete sidewalks
alone, or
turn the soil, and
sow a life together?

SEEDS

I spilt my seed on the Kalahari,
glistening sun,
never ripening.
I stood without you, and
every creature of the sand
and nearby growth watched
this pale human standing alone
as I called the Gods,
invoking your name with
an offering of children that
might have grown.

I will not kiss, taste you,
bury my love deep inside,
seeds won't sprout.
Bone crushing loneliness,
cries to an empty sky.

The afternoon on fire,
sunset's red flames
burning me
as I burn within.
Remembering your body burning,
and I spread your ashes here among the sands.

LAST LOVE

Had four loves in my life.
A bouquet of lovers:
one woman, three men.

Lost the first to dismay,
always depressed and ill,
her mind. Others to drugs,

cocaine, Prozac and rum deal a
certain and unalterable ending,
disease taking away all
physical ability to love.

I drown in self-pity,
thinking I'd always
be alone,
leaving me with a life
empty, carved by want,
sand and shells cracked,
shifting, seeking.

Till a starless blanketed night,
your light
shone my way,
ebb tide, filling the cold,
sandy canyons of my heart.

A flame burning,
a raindrop song
saying, *if there is an always*,
then I still burn.

Until you,
my last love–
join me.

SECOND CHANCE

You left me standing in hot evening sun,
brake lights blurred through tears,
burning my retinas,
dual sunspots setting on the horizon.

Should have thrown myself onto the pavement,
begged you not to go
as you drove away to your riches,
your unhappy life, away
from all that held you safe.

If a second chance comes my way,
walking around a corner like a lazy summer day,
or rushing at me like late October wind,
I will hold you in my arms,
give you my strength and never let you go,
never let your hand leave mine,
forever relishing fingertips together,
lips tracing soft lines of smiles,
and mirrored reflection of love within our eyes.

If a second chance slaps me in the face,
like a bitter winter wind, cold,
I will bundle up with you beside a roaring fire
and hibernate till spring, living off fat stores.

But if it softly lands on my shoulder,
like the flutter of avian wing
I will smile, knowing you are only one heartbeat
away,
I will sit and watch you sleep
and count the breaths we share.

Should a second chance jump in my lap,
I will hold it like a fat cat snuggled close,
kneading claws into my flesh,
nurture it, feed it, so it will never go away.

MY AGE

My age slips through my fingertips,
not holding flowers now
knowing I have not wept my despair
that I must weep to keep us
remembering
the part of you that lingers on my skin
like cream scented lotions where you lay.

At times you appear from nowhere,
your face, your perfect naked body
as a pink rose
and more beautiful.

Your scent, a smile on my lips,
a taste on my tongue,
the wind blowing my hair
surrounds me as in a room of sunlight.

Shine love upon me,
pacify my love as a vicious dog
gnawing, biting, rocking our bodies
as on the waves of the ocean,
salt of the sea and
the coming together
two pieces of one soul.

And as the winter sets upon me,
I realize I have not found that love,
that love that I thought I knew.
I have not known it as it sits in my mind
or on my tongue or my fingertips.

I will not know it, or perhaps
one late day it will be
in the mirror smiling at me, and
I will move beyond the sunlight
to a place of never-ending love.

I have had sun-soaked picnics
and kisses in the rain, thoughtful
defense and betrayals. I've had men and women
try to love me, but not as I've needed.

Perhaps I've had it all along,
I shall sit by the cliffs
see if I have passed it by and
wait for the return of the red-billed chough.

CONCLUSION

THE KNOCK

It was expected, but
what stood on the other side of
the door, a surprise to exceed
all other gifts I ever dreamed.
An entire lifetime of gifts.

You entered, working for our family.
I knew your name, nothing of what you were,
standing there in that blue-gray suit that got torn
only outshined by eyes the color of the earth.

An instant cataclysmic collision,
magnetic,
gravitational force too strong to fight,
pulled into a stream washing us together,
avoidance impossible.

As we came together, fused in embrace,
locked forever, our passion like
a solar flare.
Meteors slicing through the atmosphere
leaving streaks, marks I would have to
explain and having no explanation
other than my world had collided with yours.

We fell into each other like a wild dog of Africa
falls on an impala,
leaving not much more than bone
and heat dissipating into the heavens.
We peeled like an orange, sweet citrus
fragrance, zest and the sweet juice filled
sections of each other.

There would not be another star burst
as this one, life would never return
as before, always we would touch,
meet, love, hope we could be together.

We made the only honorable choice,
maintain the commitments we'd made,
protect others innocently floating through
space, a void created by our new world.
You with two polished stones
to carry in your pocket,
reminding you of us.

Leaving me to live on memories, bits
of news, pictures, notes, absolute
knowledge that ours is the kind of love
I have always searched for, longed to find,
dreamed of, and wanted.

Always the stream pulls me toward you,
fighting, paddling against the current,
keeping afloat just enough to continue life,
hoping to live long enough to freely
allow the stream one day to swiftly
take me to you, and
let me knock on your door.

Edgar Jay, my little rooster. Spread your wings!

ABOUT THE AUTHOR

Willis McCree was born in rural Western Kentucky and grew up on a farm. His previously published works include *When Friends Come Over*, a cookbook, and *Dark Stones I Carried*, a collection of poetry. Willis resides in Ogden, Utah.